Yesterday, Today & Tomorrow

A book about me.
Funny. Serious. Caring. Rad. Interesting. Did I really say that?
Well... until I was 12.

A guide to using

Yesterday, Today & Tomorrow
A Book About Me. Yearly Snapshots. Did I say that?

Life goes past in the blink of an eye. Precious moments come and go. Memories are made, and then fade.
This book is a treasure trove of moments written down, and deepest thoughts expressed.
It is a journal of a child growing, changing and maturing.

When your child is young, you will have to ask them the questions, and write down their answers for them.
You may even continue to do that for them all the way through the years if you like. But it's interesting watching
their handwriting change. You can ask your child all of the questions at the one time, or spread the questions out
over days or so, depending on the mood or attitude of your child ~ you'll know what I mean.

Things that your child should do for themselves in the book of memories:
- write their own name in the box provided - even if it is a scribble when they are young!
- create a drawing for the book , in the box provided - or draw it on paper, fold it and glue it into the box.
- add photos, artwork, doodles & drawings, letters, pressed flowers, stickers, inspirations etc

Please don't guide your child's answers. Let your child be honest, and raw. They are unique. There is nobody exactly like them on the earth! And you'll look back at the answers filled with love.

" You will never have this day with your child again.
Tomorrow they'll be a little older than they we're today.
This day is a gift. Breathe and notice.
Smell and touch them; study their faces
and little feet and pay attention.
RELISH THE CHARMS of THE PRESENT.

Enjoy today. It will be over before you know it."

~ Jen Hatmaker

And then you arrived,
and everything changed.

Announcing...

THE BIRTH OF

Born on this day _____

of the month _____

in the year of _____

at the time of _____

weighing _____

length _____

hair colour _____

eye colour _____

to the proud parents, my mum and dad,

When I was 1

This is me!

What words describe you? _____

This is how I write my name.

My nickname is _____

My most used facial expression _____

_____

_____

My first smile was at _____

I rolled over at _____

I sat up at _____

I was aged _____ when I first stood up against furniture.

I started to walk at _____

My first word was _____

Other words I use _____

_____

_____

My most special toy is _____

because _____

_____

The shoes that I really like are? _____

I like them because _____

_____

What type of weather do I like the best? _____

I don't like _____

_____

The number one outdoor activity that I like to do is _____

_____

The things that make me giggle are _____

_____

_____

When I am excited, I _____

_____

The indoor game activity that I like to do is _____

The music that I like to listen to is _____

For breakfast, I enjoy eating _____

_____

A delicious lunch for me is _____
I love to eat _____ for dinner!
A book or a story that I really, really like is _____

_____

I like to drink _____
A movie that I love to watch is (if I'm allowed) _____
Do I watch television? yes/no. If yes, I like to watch _____

_____

The healthy food that is the most delicious for me is _____

_____

I also like to eat _____

_____

I like to say _____

_____

The colour I adore is _____

Favourite fruit _____

Favourite vegetable _____

Sweets I like to eat _____

If I could have more of something, I would have more of _____

because _____

If I could have less of something, I would have less of _____

because _____

My friends are _____

_____

_____

I think that bath time is _____

Animals I love: _____

_____

I like to go to _____

because _____

I am very good at _____

_____

I like to help with _____

_____

I don't like _____

_____

_____

Things I did - funny, serious, adventurous, dangerous, brilliant, heartwarming

My height at the age of one is ____________

My favourite thing to do this year, was ______________________________

Hopes, dreams or prayers for me

One from Mum: _____

_____

_____

One from Dad: _____

_____

_____

One from _____ : _____

_____

_____

A drawing

Photographs & Stuff

My handprint

When I was 2

This is me!

What words describe you? _____

This is how I write my name.

My nickname is:
From Mum: _____
From Dad: _____
My most used facial expression _____
_____
_____

My word list _____
_____
_____
_____
_____

Phrases I like to use _____
_____
_____

My most special toy is _____
because _____
The shoes that I really like are? _____
What type of weather do I like the best? _____
I don't like _____
_____

The number one outdoor activity that I like to do is _____

_____

_____

The thing that makes me giggle is _____

_____

_____

When I am excited, I _____

_____

The indoor game activity that I like to do is _____

The music that I like to listen to is _____

_____

For breakfast, I enjoy eating _____

_____

A delicious lunch for me is _____
I love to eat _____ for dinner!
A book or a story that I really, really like is _____

_____

I like to drink _____
A movie that I love to watch is (if I'm allowed) _____
Do I watch television? yes/no If yes, I like to watch _____

_____

The healthy food that is the most delicious for me is _____

_____

I also like to eat _____

_____

I like to _____

_____

_____

The colour I adore is _____

Favourite fruit _____

Favourite vegetable _____

Sweets I like to eat _____

If I could have more of something, I would have more of _____

because _____

_____

If I could have less of something, I would have less of _____

because _____

_____

My friends are _____

_____

_____

_____

I would like to thank Mum for _____

_____

and I would like to thank Dad for _____

_____

What I like about myself is _____

_____

_____

If I could own any pet, I would choose a _____

because _____

If I could choose any musical instrument to play, I would choose a _____

_____

The sport that I love to play is _____

I like to help at home by _____

_____

My height at the age of two is _____

My favourite thing this year, was _____

My hopes, dreams or prayers

One for me: _____

_____

_____

One for my family: _____

_____

_____

One for the world: _____

_____

_____

A drawing

My handprint

When I was 3

This is me!

How would you describe yourself? _____

This is how I write my name.

My nickname is _____

_____

My best age so far is _____
because _____

_____

My most special toy is _____
because_____

_____

The shoes that I really like are? _____
I like them because _____

_____

Will I drive a car or motorbike when I grow up? _____
The colour of it will be _____
Things I don't like _____

_____

_____

because _____
What type of weather do I like the best? _____
because _____

The number one outdoor game that I like to play is _____

_____

If I could change something about myself, it would be? _____

_____

When I grow up I want to be a _____

The indoor game that I like to play is _____

_____

The music that I like to listen to is _____

For breakfast, I enjoy eating _____

A delicious lunch for me is _____

I love to eat _____ for dinner!

Snacks I like to eat are _____

_____

A book or a story that I really, really like is _____

_____

I like to drink _____

The movie that I love to watch is _____

On television, or other technology, I like to watch _____

_____

_____

The healthy food that is the most delicious for me is _____

I also like to eat _____

_____

I like to say _____

_____

Things I like to do _____

_____

_____

The colour I adore is _____

Favourite fruit _____

Favourite vegetable _____

Sweets I like to eat _____

If I could have more of something, I would have more of _____

because _____

_____

If I could have less of something, I would have less of _____

because _____

_____

My friends are _____

_____

_____

I would like to thank Mum for _____

and I would like to thank Dad for _____

What I like about myself is _____

_____

If I could own any pet, I would choose a _____

because _____

If I could choose any musical instrument to play, I would choose a _____

The sport that I love to play is _____

I like to help at home by _____

_____

Things I did – funny, serious, adventurous, dangerous, brilliant, heartwarming

My height at the age of three is _____

My favourite thing this year, was _____

My hopes, dreams or prayers

One for me: _____

_____

_____

One for my family: _____

_____

One for the world: _____

_____

One for my friends: _____

_____

_____

A drawing

Photographs & Stuff

dream big

When I was 4

This is me!

How would you describe yourself? _____

This is how I write my name.

My nickname is _____

My best age so far is _____
because _____

_____

_____

My most special toy is _____
because_____

_____

The shoes that I really like are? _____
I like them because _____

_____

Will I drive a car or motorbike when I grow up? _____
The colour of it will be _____
Things I don't like _____

_____

_____

because _____
What type of weather do I like the best? _____
because _____

The number one outdoor game that I like to play is _____

_____

If I could change something about myself, it would be? _____

_____

When I grow up I want to be a _____
The indoor game that I like to play is _____

_____

The music that I like to listen to is _____
For breakfast, I enjoy eating _____
A delicious lunch for me is _____
I love to eat _____ for dinner!
Snacks I like to eat are _____

_____

A book or a story that I really, really like is _____

_____

I like to drink _____
The movie that I love to watch is _____
On television, or other technology, I like to watch _____

_____

_____

The healthy food that is the most delicious for me is _____
I also like to eat _____

_____

I like to say _____

_____

Things I like to do _____

_____

_____

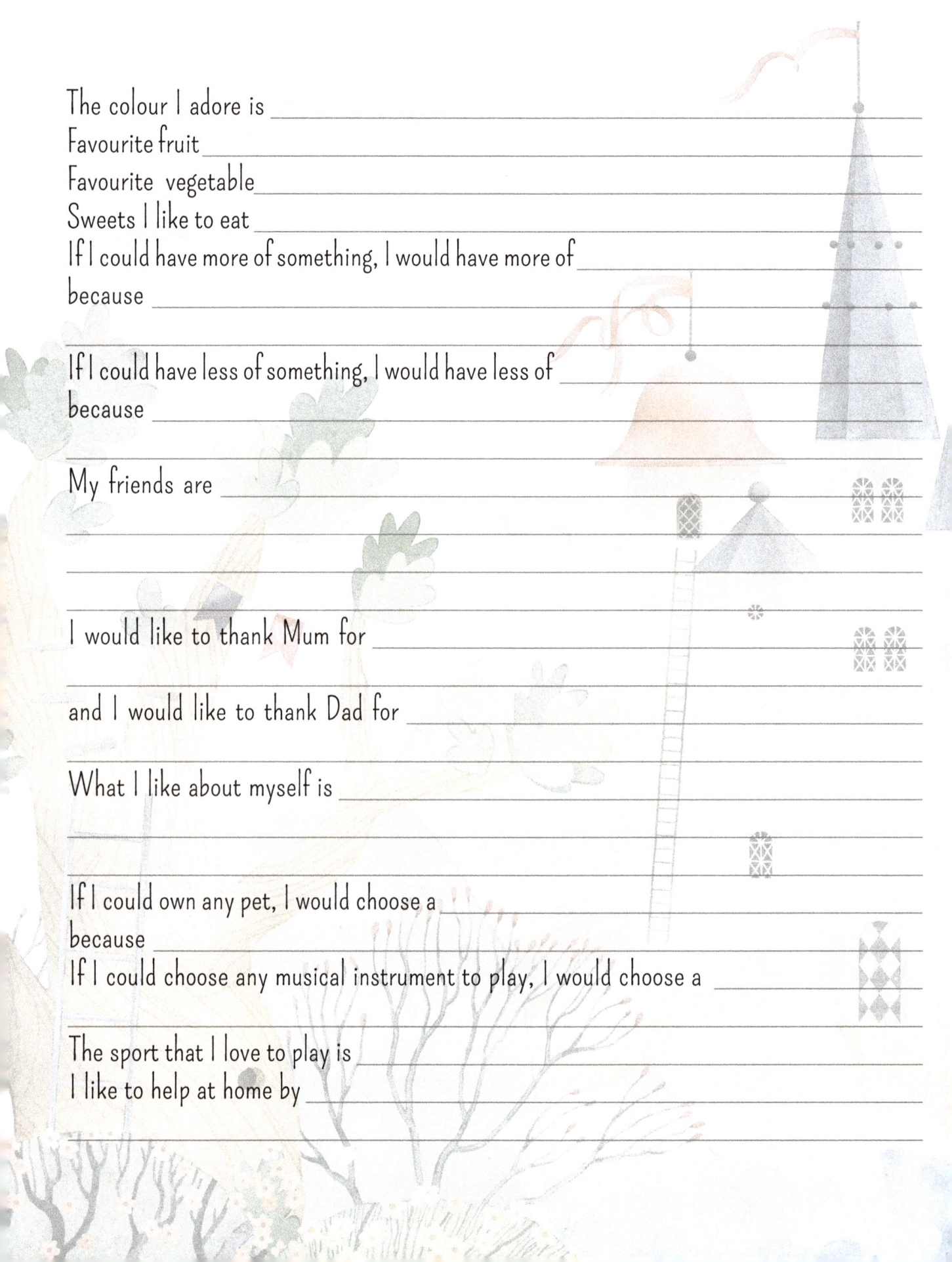

The colour I adore is _____

Favourite fruit _____

Favourite vegetable _____

Sweets I like to eat _____

If I could have more of something, I would have more of _____

because _____

_____

If I could have less of something, I would have less of _____

because _____

_____

My friends are _____

_____

_____

_____

I would like to thank Mum for _____

_____

and I would like to thank Dad for _____

What I like about myself is _____

_____

_____

If I could own any pet, I would choose a _____

because _____

If I could choose any musical instrument to play, I would choose a _____

_____

The sport that I love to play is _____

I like to help at home by _____

_____

My height at the age of four is _____
My favourite thing this year, was _____

My hopes, dreams or prayers

One for me: _____

_____

One for my family: _____

_____

One for the world: _____

_____

One for my friends: _____

_____

A drawing

ADVENTURE

ADVENTURE

When I was 5

This is me!

How would you describe yourself? _____

This is how I write my name.

My nickname is _____

My best age so far is _____
because _____

_____

My most special toy is _____
because_____

_____

The shoes that I really like are? _____
I like them because _____

_____

Will I drive a car or motorbike when I grow up? _____
The colour of it will be _____
Things I don't like _____

_____

_____

because _____
What type of weather do I like the best? _____
because _____

The number one outdoor game that I like to play is _____

_____

If I could change something about myself, it would be? _____

_____

When I grow up I want to be a _____
The indoor game that I like to play is _____

_____

The music that I like to listen to is _____
For breakfast, I enjoy eating _____
A delicious lunch for me is _____
I love to eat _____ for dinner!
Snacks I like to eat are _____

_____

A book or a story that I really, really like is _____

_____

I like to drink _____
The movie that I love to watch is _____
On television, or other technology, I like to watch _____

_____

_____

The healthy food that is the most delicious for me is _____
I also like to eat _____

_____

I like to say _____

_____

Things I like to do _____

_____

_____

The colour I adore is _____

Favourite fruit _____

Favourite vegetable _____

Sweets I like to eat _____

If I could have more of something, I would have more of _____

because _____

_____

If I could have less of something, I would have less of _____

because _____

_____

My friends are _____

_____

_____

_____

I would like to thank Mum for _____

and I would like to thank Dad for _____

What I like about myself is _____

_____

If I could own any pet, I would choose a _____

because _____

If I could choose any musical instrument to play, I would choose a _____

_____

The sport that I love to play is _____

I like to help at home by _____

_____

Things I did – funny, serious, adventurous, dangerous, brilliant, heartwarming

My height at the age of five is _____
My favourite memory this year, was _____

My hopes, dreams or prayers

One for me: _____

_____

One for my family: _____

_____

One for the world: _____

_____

One for my friends: _____

_____

_____

A drawing

Photographs & Stuff

When I was 6

This is me!

How would you describe yourself? _____

This is how I write my name.

My nickname is _____

_____

My best age so far is _____
because _____

_____

_____

My most special toy is _____
because_____

_____

The shoes that I really like are? _____
I like them because _____

_____

Will I drive a car or motorbike when I grow up? _____
The colour of it will be _____
Things I don't like _____

_____

_____

because _____
What type of weather do I like the best? _____
because _____

The number one outdoor game that I like to play is _____

_____

If I could change something about myself, it would be? _____

_____

When I grow up I want to be a _____
The indoor game that I like to play is _____

_____

The music that I like to listen to is _____
For breakfast, I enjoy eating _____
A delicious lunch for me is _____
I love to eat _____ for dinner!
Snacks I like to eat are _____

A book or a story that I really, really like is _____

_____

I like to drink _____
The movie that I love to watch is _____
On television, or other technology, I like to watch _____

_____

_____

The healthy food that is the most delicious for me is _____
I also like to eat _____

_____

I like to say _____

Things I like to do _____

_____

_____

The colour I adore is _____

Favourite fruit _____

Favourite vegetable _____

Sweets I like to eat _____

If I could have more of something, I would have more of _____

because _____

_____

If I could have less of something, I would have less of _____

because _____

_____

My friends are _____

_____

_____

_____

I would like to thank Mum for _____

and I would like to thank Dad for _____

What I like about myself is _____

_____

_____

If I could own any pet, I would choose a _____

because _____

If I could choose any musical instrument to play, I would choose a _____

_____

The sport that I love to play is _____

I like to help at home by _____

_____

Things I did – funny, serious, adventurous, dangerous, brilliant, heartwarming

My height at the age of six is _____

My favourite memory this year, was _____

My hopes, dreams or prayers

One for me: _____

_____

One for my family: _____

_____

One for the world: _____

_____

One for my friends: _____

_____

A drawing

When I was 7

This is me!

How would you describe yourself? _____

This is how I write my name.

My nickname is _____

_____

My best age so far is _____
because _____

_____

_____

My most special toy is _____
because_____

_____

The shoes that I really like are? _____
I like them because _____

_____

Will I drive a car or motorbike when I grow up? _____
The colour of it will be _____
Things I don't like _____

_____

_____

because _____
What type of weather do I like the best? _____
because _____

The number one outdoor game that I like to play is _____

If I could change something about myself, it would be? _____

When I grow up I want to be a _____
The indoor game that I like to play is _____

The music that I like to listen to is _____
For breakfast, I enjoy eating _____
A delicious lunch for me is _____
I love to eat _____ for dinner!
Snacks I like to eat are _____

A book or a story that I really, really like is _____

I like to drink _____
The movie that I love to watch is _____
On television, or other technology, I like to watch _____

The healthy food that is the most delicious for me is _____
I also like to eat _____

I like to say _____

Things I like to do _____

The colour I adore is _____

Favourite fruit _____

Favourite vegetable _____

Sweets I like to eat _____

If I could have more of something, I would have more of _____

because _____

_____

If I could have less of something, I would have less of _____

because _____

_____

My friends are _____

_____

_____

_____

I would like to thank Mum for _____

_____

and I would like to thank Dad for _____

_____

What I like about myself is _____

_____

_____

If I could own any pet, I would choose a _____

because _____

If I could choose any musical instrument to play, I would choose a _____

_____

The sport that I love to play is _____

I like to help at home by _____

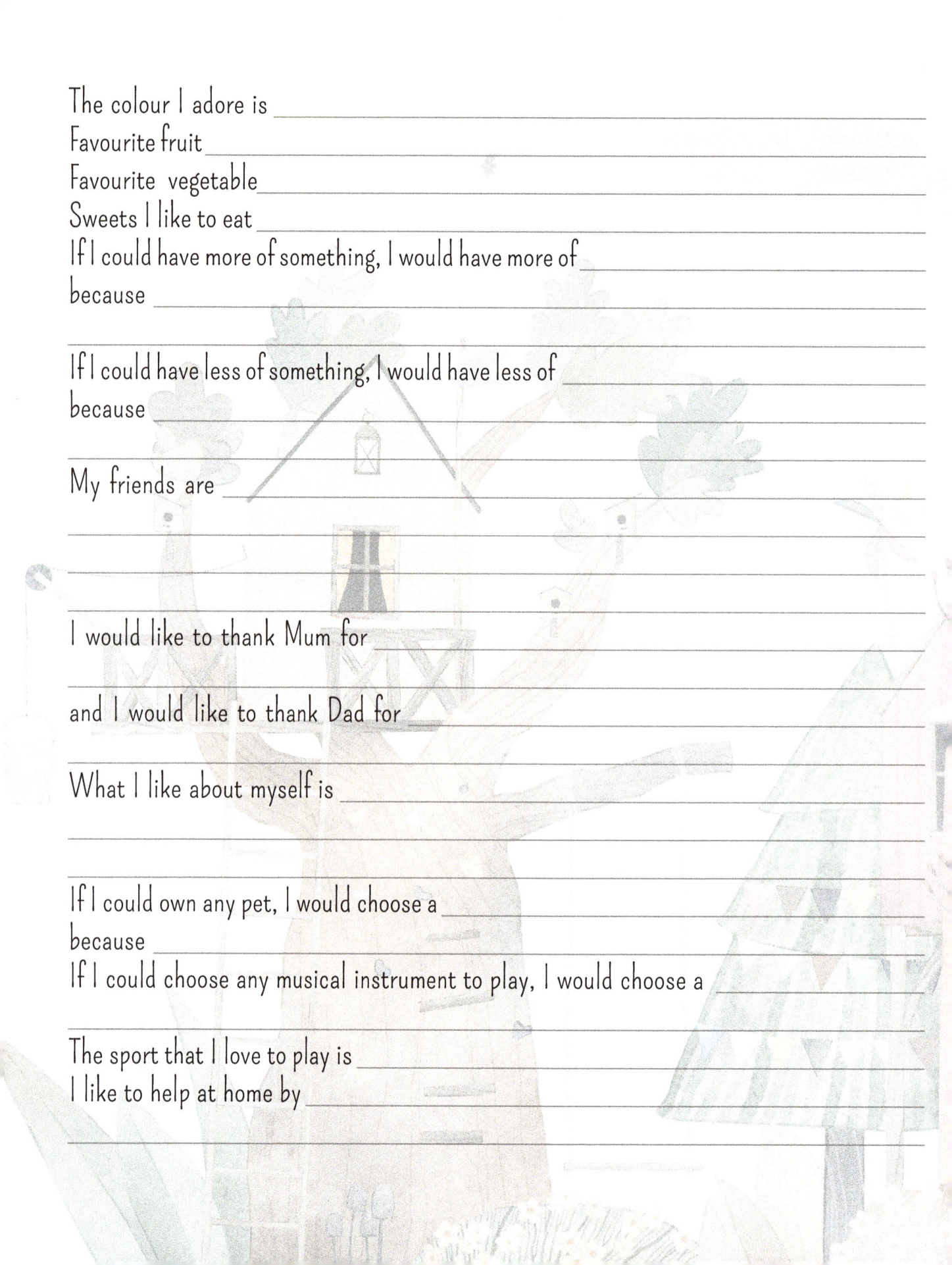

_____

Things I did - funny, serious, adventurous, dangerous, brilliant, heartwarming

My height at the age of seven is _____
My favourite memory this year, was _____

My hopes, dreams or prayers

One for me: _____

_____

One for my family: _____

_____

One for the world: _____

_____

One for my friends: _____

_____

A drawing

dream
big

dream
big

PIRATE

dream
big

dream
big

N S

P

dream
big

A+N=♡

PIRATE

My handprint

When I was 8

This is me!

How would you describe yourself? _____

This is how I write my name.

My nickname is _____

My best age so far is _____
because _____
_____

My most special toy is _____
because _____

The shoes that I really like are? _____
I like them because _____

Will I drive a car or motorbike when I grow up? _____
The colour of it will be _____
Things I don't like _____
_____

because _____
What type of weather do I like the best? _____
because _____

The number one outdoor game that I like to play is _____

_____

If I could change something about myself, it would be? _____

_____

When I grow up I want to be a _____
The indoor game that I like to play is _____

_____

The music that I like to listen to is _____
For breakfast, I enjoy eating _____
A delicious lunch for me is _____
I love to eat _____ for dinner!
Snacks I like to eat are _____

_____

A book or a story that I really, really like is _____

_____

I like to drink _____
The movie that I love to watch is _____
On television, or other technology, I like to watch _____

_____

The healthy food that is the most delicious for me is _____
I also like to eat _____

_____

I like to say _____

Things I like to do _____

_____

_____

The colour I adore is _____

Favourite fruit_____

Favourite vegetable_____

Sweets I like to eat _____

If I could have more of something, I would have more of _____

because _____

_____

If I could have less of something, I would have less of _____

because _____

_____

My friends are _____

_____

_____

_____

I would like to thank Mum for _____

and I would like to thank Dad for _____

What I like about myself is _____

_____

_____

If I could own any pet, I would choose a _____

because _____

If I could choose any musical instrument to play, I would choose a _____

_____

The sport that I love to play is _____

I like to help at home by _____

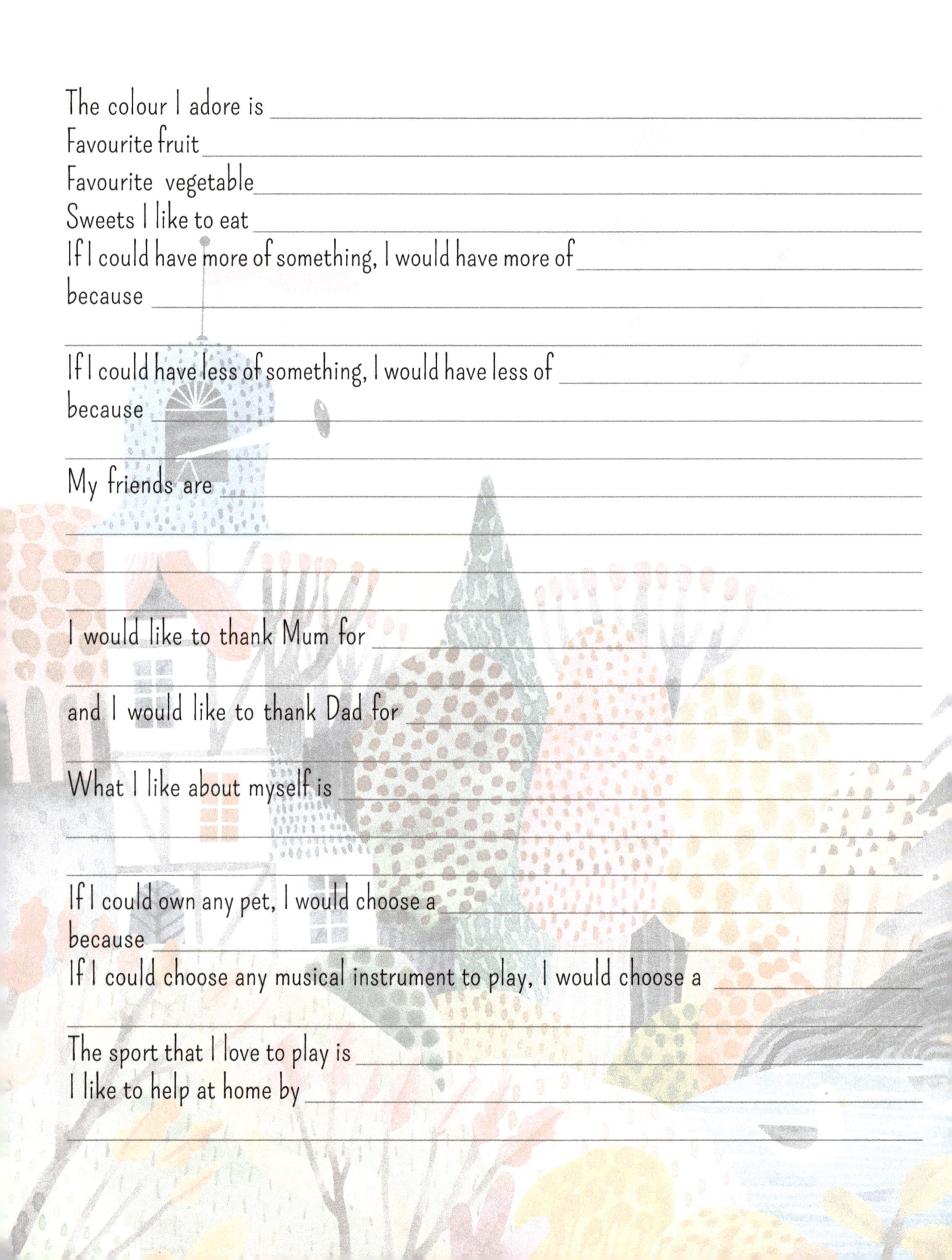

_____

Things I did – funny, serious, adventurous, dangerous, brilliant, heartwarming

My height at the age of eight is _____

My favourite memory this year, was _____

My hopes, dreams or prayers

One for me: _____

_____

One for my family: _____

_____

One for the world: _____

_____

One for my friends: _____

_____

A drawing

Photographs, a letter to myself & other stuff

When I was 9

This is me!

How would you describe yourself? _____

This is how I write my name.

My nickname is _____

My best age so far is _____
because _____

_____

My most special toy is _____
because _____

_____

The shoes that I really like are? _____
I like them because _____

_____

Will I drive a car or motorbike when I grow up? _____
The colour of it will be _____
Things I don't like _____

_____

_____
because _____
What type of weather do I like the best? _____
because _____

The number one outdoor game that I like to play is _____

_____

If I could change something about myself, it would be? _____

_____

When I grow up I want to be a _____

The indoor game that I like to play is _____

_____

The music that I like to listen to is _____

For breakfast, I enjoy eating _____

A delicious lunch for me is _____

I love to eat _____ for dinner!

Snacks I like to eat are _____

_____

A book or a story that I really, really like is _____

_____

I like to drink _____

The movie that I love to watch is _____

On television, or other technology, I like to watch _____

_____

_____

The healthy food that is the most delicious for me is _____

I also like to eat _____

_____

I like to say _____

_____

Things I like to do _____

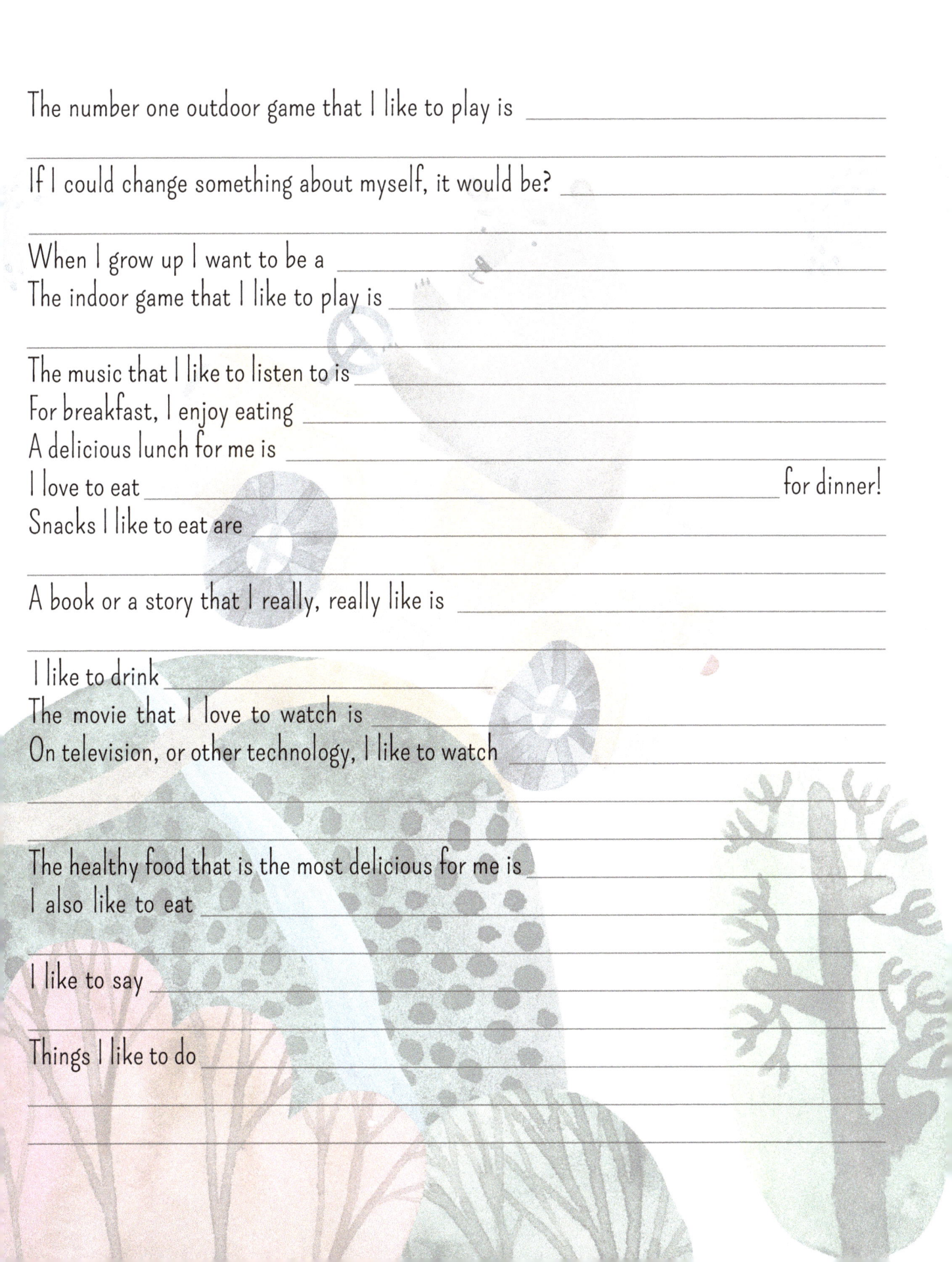

_____

_____

The colour I adore is _____

Favourite fruit _____

Favourite vegetable _____

Sweets I like to eat _____

If I could have more of something, I would have more of _____

because _____

_____

If I could have less of something, I would have less of _____

because _____

_____

My friends are _____

_____

_____

_____

I would like to thank Mum for _____

_____

and I would like to thank Dad for _____

_____

What I like about myself is _____

_____

_____

If I could own any pet, I would choose a _____

because _____

If I could choose any musical instrument to play, I would choose a _____

_____

The sport that I love to play is _____

I like to help at home by _____

_____

Things I did - funny, serious, adventurous, dangerous, brilliant, heartwarming

_____

_____

_____

_____

_____

_____

_____

_____

_____

_____

_____

_____

_____

_____

_____

_____

_____

_____

My height at the age of nine is _____

My favourite memory this year, was _____

_____

My hopes, dreams or prayers

One for me: _____

_____

_____

One for my family: _____

_____

_____

One for the world: _____

_____

_____

One for my friends: _____

_____

_____

A drawing

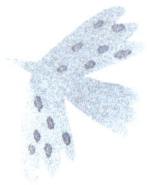

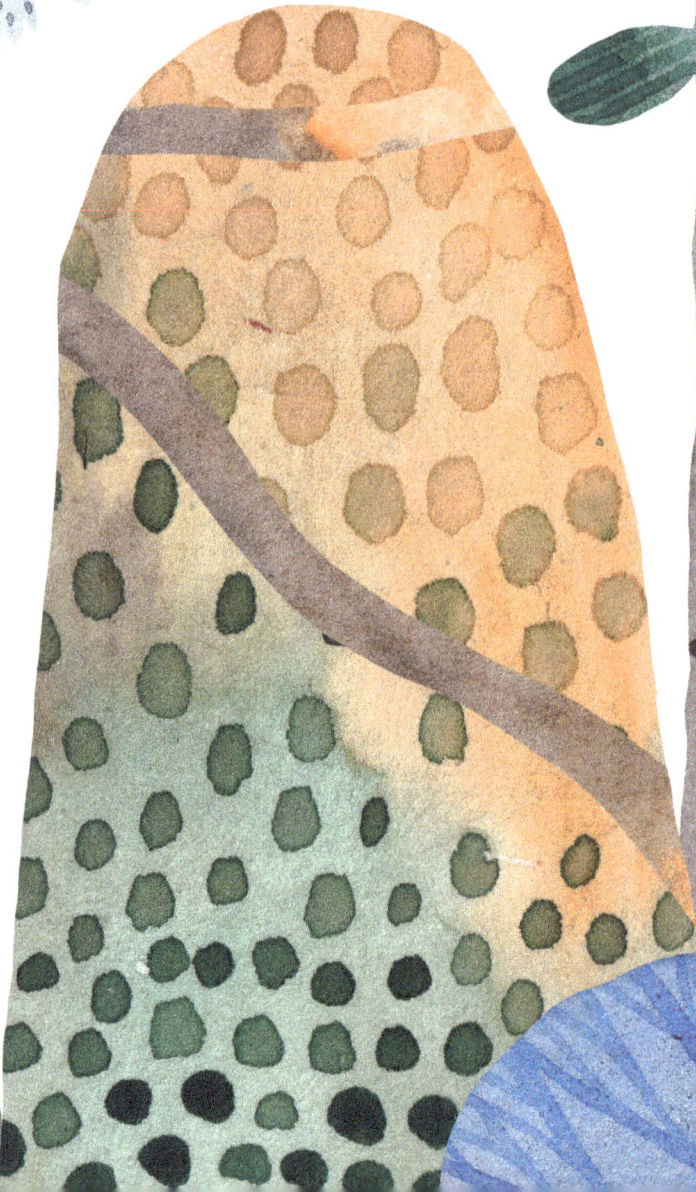

When I was 10

This is me!

How would you describe yourself? _____

This is how I write my name.

My nickname is _____

_____

My best age so far is _____
because _____

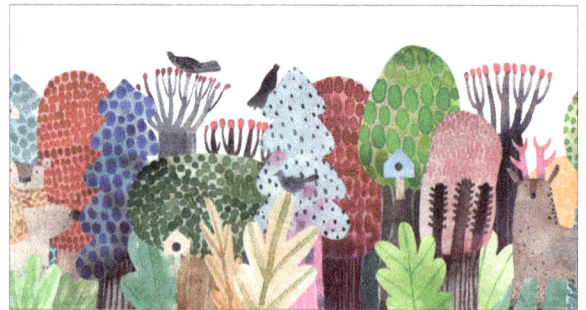

_____

My most special toy is _____
because_____

_____

The shoes that I really like are? _____
I like them because _____

_____

Will I drive a car or motorbike when I grow up? _____
The colour of it will be _____
Things I don't like _____

_____

because _____
What type of weather do I like the best? _____
because _____

The number one outdoor game that I like to play is _____

_____

If I could change something about myself, it would be? _____

_____

When I grow up I want to be a _____
The indoor game that I like to play is _____

_____

The music that I like to listen to is _____
For breakfast, I enjoy eating _____
A delicious lunch for me is _____
I love to eat _____ for dinner!
Snacks I like to eat are _____

_____

A book or a story that I really, really like is _____

_____

I like to drink _____
The movie that I love to watch is _____
On television, or other technology, I like to watch _____

_____

The healthy food that is the most delicious for me is _____
I also like to eat _____

_____

I like to say _____

_____

Things I like to do _____

_____

_____

The colour I adore is _____

Favourite fruit _____

Favourite vegetable _____

Sweets I like to eat _____

If I could have more of something, I would have more of _____

because _____

_____

If I could have less of something, I would have less of _____

because _____

_____

My friends are _____

_____

_____

_____

I would like to thank Mum for _____

_____

and I would like to thank Dad for _____

_____

What I like about myself is _____

_____

_____

If I could own any pet, I would choose a _____

because _____

If I could choose any musical instrument to play, I would choose a _____

_____

The sport that I love to play is _____

I like to help at home by _____

_____

Things I did - funny, serious, adventurous, dangerous, brilliant, heartwarming

My height at the age of ten is _____

My favourite memory this year, was _____

My hopes, dreams or prayers

One for me: _____

_____

One for my family: _____

_____

One for the world: _____

_____

One for my friends: _____

_____

_____

A drawing

Photographs, a letter to myself & other stuff

When I was 11

This is me!

How would you describe yourself? _____

This is how I write my name.

My nickname is _____

_____

My best age so far is _____
because _____
_____

My most special toy is _____
because_____
_____

The shoes that I really like are? _____
I like them because _____
_____

Will I drive a car or motorbike when I grow up? _____
The colour of it will be _____
Things I don't like _____
_____
_____
because _____
What type of weather do I like the best? _____
because _____

The number one outdoor game that I like to play is _____

_____

If I could change something about myself, it would be? _____

_____

When I grow up I want to be a _____

The indoor game that I like to play is _____

_____

The music that I like to listen to is _____

For breakfast, I enjoy eating _____

A delicious lunch for me is _____

I love to eat _____ for dinner!

Snacks I like to eat are _____

_____

A book or a story that I really, really like is _____

_____

I like to drink _____

The movie that I love to watch is _____

On television, or other technology, I like to watch _____

_____

_____

The healthy food that is the most delicious for me is _____

I also like to eat _____

_____

I like to say _____

_____

Things I like to do _____

_____

_____

The colour I adore is _____

Favourite fruit _____

Favourite vegetable _____

Sweets I like to eat _____

If I could have more of something, I would have more of _____

because _____

_____

If I could have less of something, I would have less of _____

because _____

_____

My friends are _____

_____

_____

_____

I would like to thank Mum for _____

_____

and I would like to thank Dad for _____

_____

What I like about myself is _____

_____

If I could own any pet, I would choose a _____

because _____

If I could choose any musical instrument to play, I would choose a _____

_____

The sport that I love to play is _____

I like to help at home by _____

_____

Things I did – funny, serious, adventurous, dangerous, brilliant, heartwarming

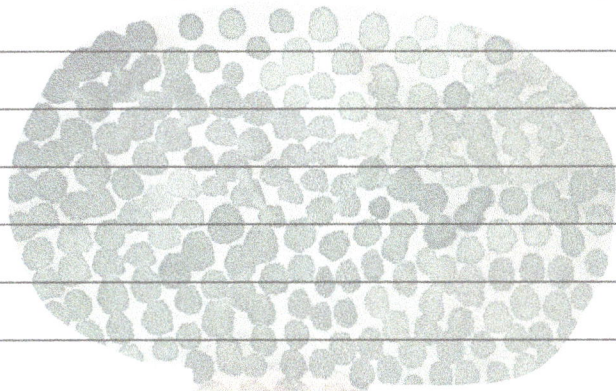

My height at the age of eleven is _____

My favourite memory this year, was _____

My hopes, dreams or prayers

One for me: _____

_____

One for my family: _____

_____

One for the world: _____

_____

One for my friends: _____

_____

A drawing

Photographs, a letter to myself & other stuff

When I was 12

This is me!

How would you describe yourself? _____

This is how I write my name.

My nickname is _____

_____

My best age so far is _____
because _____

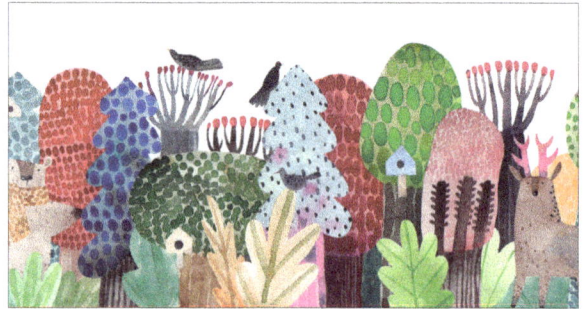

_____

My most special toy is _____
because _____

_____

The shoes that I really like are? _____
I like them because _____

_____

Will I drive a car or motorbike when I grow up? _____
The colour of it will be _____
Things I don't like _____

_____

_____

because _____
What type of weather do I like the best? _____
because _____

The number one outdoor game that I like to play is _____

_____

If I could change something about myself, it would be? _____

_____

When I grow up I want to be a _____

The indoor game that I like to play is _____

_____

The music that I like to listen to is _____

For breakfast, I enjoy eating _____

A delicious lunch for me is _____

I love to eat _____ for dinner!

Snacks I like to eat are _____

_____

A book or a story that I really, really like is _____

_____

I like to drink _____

The movie that I love to watch is _____

On television, or other technology, I like to watch _____

_____

_____

The healthy food that is the most delicious for me is _____

I also like to eat _____

_____

I like to say _____

_____

Things I like to do _____

_____

_____

The colour I adore is _____

Favourite fruit _____

Favourite vegetable _____

Sweets I like to eat _____

If I could have more of something, I would have more of _____

because _____

_____

If I could have less of something, I would have less of _____

because _____

_____

My friends are _____

_____

_____

_____

I would like to thank Mum for _____

_____

and I would like to thank Dad for _____

What I like about myself is _____

_____

If I could own any pet, I would choose a _____

because _____

If I could choose any musical instrument to play, I would choose a _____

_____

The sport that I love to play is _____

I like to help at home by _____

_____

Things I did - funny, serious, adventurous, dangerous, brilliant, heartwarming

_____

_____

_____

_____

_____

_____

_____

_____

_____

_____

_____

_____

_____

_____

_____

_____

_____

_____

_____

My height at the age of twelve is _____

My favourite memory this year, was _____

_____

My hopes, dreams or prayers

One for me: _____
_____
_____

One for my family: _____
_____
_____

One for the world: _____
_____
_____

One for my friends: _____
_____
_____

A drawing

Photographs, a letter to myself & other stuff

Yesterday, Today & Tomorrow
A Book About Me. Yearly Snapshots. Did I say that?
2025 ©Julieann Wallace

Published by King's Ink Publishing 2025
kingsinkpublishing@outlook.com

PROUDLY

HI

Human Intelligence.
Creativity. Imagination. Heart. Soul. Original.

Cover Art by Bukhavets (Adobe Stock)
Cover design by King's Ink Publishing
Interior Layout by King's Ink Publishing
Interior Art by by Bukhavets (Adobe Stock)
Trees by Kudryashka (123RF)
Hands by Scusi (123RF)

ISBN: 978-0-6451581-3-7 (hard cover)

About the Author

Julieann is a mum of three, Grams of one, writer, artist, and teacher who tries not to scare her cat, Claude Monet, or her mini dachshund, Pablo Picasso, with her terrible cello playing.
Her teaching career spans over 35 years, and when she taught primary students, as an end-of-year gift for parents of the students in her classes, she would create a memory book of each student. Included in the memory book was a questionnaire, much like this book, which the parents adored.

Julieann is also an author of picture books, middle grade books, YA books and adult fiction.
You can find them here at www.julieannwallaceauthor.com

Be sure to check out Julieann's newborn baby books, 'Forever and a Day ~ love, Mama'

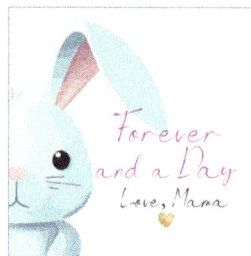

The First 12 Years. A Reflection. A Letter.

www.ingramcontent.com/pod-product-compliance
Lightning Source LLC
Chambersburg PA
CBHW040315100426
42811CB00012B/1448